ZENOVIA CATERING
PRESENTS:

CUISINE
ALÀ
KIDS

A FAMILY COOKBOOK FOR CHILDREN AND THEIR ADULT HELPERS

Written by: Janet Christon
Photos by: Evan Christon

ISBN: 0–9768378–0–3

Printed in the United States of America
Bloomington, Indiana

This book is printed on acid-free paper.

CAK
Publishing

A Message from the Author:

"Young Minds; Young Chefs"

Kids are wonderful people. They are funny, spontaneous and brutally honest! They also know what they like and dislike.

Encouraging a child's interest in cooking and baking at a young age can be most beneficial to their future, while creating lots of family fun.

No matter what career choices a child ultimately makes, cooking encourages self-reliance and a necessity for living and eating well.

Planning and preparing meals together ensure some extra quality time for you and your child, while involving them in various eating experiences (some their choices, some yours).

Creating different and delicious menus can be an exciting and memorable experience for the entire family.

I know from personal experience, it's a labor of love.

Janet Christon
Of Zenovia Catering

A DEDICATION FROM THE AUTHOR
JANET CHRISTON:

This cookbook is dedicated to my Dad, Philip Daston, who has been my culinary inspiration from the beginning.

Thanks, Pop!

SAFETY FIRST:

Adult Helpers:

While cooking and baking can be great fun, it can also be dangerous if an adult helper does not properly supervise a child.

Children must understand that a great deal of caution is involved in using the kitchen and it's appliances. Therefore, the adults involved in these projects must assume full responsibility for the safety of their children by not allowing them to operate difficult or dangerous appliances and gadgets by themselves. It is also the responsibility of the adult helper to decide when their child is of proper age to do so.

** Hint: It is wise to keep a kitchen fire extinguisher and a First
Aid kit handy.

HINTS:

Help your children with their math. Have them do the measuring.

Let the kids set the table. You'd be surprised as to how creative they can be.

Let the kids choose salad ingredients and mix their own dressings.

Let the children help with the grocery shopping. Kids eat healthier today and with their suggestions and your input you can create some fun and good-for-you menus.

Kid Chefs:

Before you begin

Please read over each safety rule
       Wash your hands and keep things clean
           Safety in the kitchen is really cool!

By kid chef: Lorin Richardson

1. Always have an adult in the kitchen with you.

2. Never use kitchen appliances or sharp objects unless an adult is with you.

3. When handling hot foods, wear kitchen mitts.

4. Always wash your hands before and after handling food.

5. Make your time in the kitchen safe and fun

CLEANLINESS:

Cleanliness is vital when preparing food. Hands should be washed before, during and after meal preparation. All utensils, bowls, dishes, pots, pans and cutting boards should also be cleaned.

Countertops can carry germs. Avoid cutting or preparing foods directly on them. Use cutting boards and wash them well.

TABLE OF CONTENTS

CHAPTER 1

KIDS SPEAK OUT!!!!!!!!!

We surveyed a group of kids ranging in ages and found that some of their favorite foods were not as common as you might think.

We included kid-tested recipes for all of them:

Nicole, age 11: Giant Shrimp Cocktail with red sauce
Zena, age 4: Chicken and Vegetable Soup
Lorin, age 15: Mac & Cheese
Melanie, age 6: Chicken Wings with dipping sauces
Katherine, age 10: Bow-Tie pasta with tomato sauce
Gregory, age 12: Turkey Subs
Katie, age 12: Spaghetti and Meatballs
Michael, age 13: Turkey Burgers
Matthew, age 9: Vanilla and Chocolate Pudding Parfait
Victoria and Catherine, ages 6 and 4: Greek Butter Cookies
Athena, age 5: Mini-Pizzas
Nicholas, age 10: Nachos Supreme

NICOLES GIANT SHRIMP COCKTAIL WITH SPICY RED SAUCE

Adult Helpers:

Ready cooked shrimp is worth a little extra cost to avoid the shelling, deveining and boiling. The spicy red sauce is easy to make and assembling the cocktail is fun.

Serves 4

Ingredients:

24 large cooked shrimp
Lettuce leaves
Spicy red sauce (recipe follows)

Spicy Red Sauce:

1 cup Ketchup
2 tsp. Chili sauce
2 tsp. Balsamic vinegar

KIDS:

Stir sauce ingredients in mixing bowl. Set aside.

Assemble large shrimp in pretty stemmed glasses with the lettuce lining the bottoms. Spoon the spicy red sauce in the middle for easy dipping.

ZENAS CHICKEN AND VEGETABLE SOUP

Our 4 year old loves helping mommy with this easy and delicious chicken soup.

You can purchase cooked chicken strips at your local supermarket.

Serves 4-6

Ingredients:

4 cups chicken broth
2 cups water
1/2 tsp. black pepper
1 cup small pasta shells. elbows, orzo, rice or noodles
1 16-ounce package frozen mixed vegetables
2 cups cooked chicken strips or chicken sausage cut in 1-inch cubes
2 tablespoons chopped fresh parsley

In a large pot combine broth, water and pepper. Bring to boil and stir in pasta. Return to boiling, lower heat to simmer, uncovered, for 5 minutes. Stir in frozen vegetables and simmer until vegetable and pasta are tender. Stir in cooked diced chicken and heat through. Salt to taste.

NICHOLAS NACHOS SUPREME

ADULTS:

This is a great recipe for homemade nachos or you may purchase store bought tortilla chips and ready-made guacamole.

Ingredients:

1 pkg. tortillas (corn or flour)
Canola or vegetable oil for deep frying

Adult Helpers:

Cut tortillas into quarters. Heat oil in deep fat fryer or deep skillet to 325 degrees. Add tortilla pieces, a few at a time, and fry, turning often until golden brown and crisp. Using a slotted spoon, remove chips from oil and drain on paper towels.

KIDS:

Tomato Salsa (have adult helper assist with chopping)

1 can diced tomatoes, drained
1 small can of corn, drained
1/3 cup diced red onions
2 tablespoons diced red bell pepper
1 tsp. lime juice
1 tablespoon of chopped cilantro
Salt to taste

Combine all ingredients in a bowl and mix well with spoon.

Melted Cheese Sauce

1 cup shredded cheddar cheese
2 drops hot pepper sauce

Combine in a microwave safe bowl and heat until cheese is melted, 30 seconds at a time. Stir often.

MELANIES BAKED CHICKEN WINGS WITH DIPPING SAUCES

16-20 chicken wings

Adult Helpers:

Rinse chicken wings; pat dry with paper towels. Cut off and discard tips. Cut wings at joints or leave whole as desired. Bake on ungreased baking sheet in 325 degree oven for about 25-30 minutes.

KIDS AND ADULTS:

Prepare sauce of your choice or use one of ours.

Cherry Sauce:

One 1 pound can pitted tart red cherries with juice
1/2 cup sugar
2 tablespoons cornstarch

Combine ingredients in blender or food processor. Pour into saucepan and heat, stirring constantly, until thick and bubbly. Reduce heat and simmer for 1 to 2 minutes. Let cool.

Plum Sauce:

1 12 ounce jar plum preserves
2 tablespoons white vinegar
2 tablespoons honey
1 tablespoon brown sugar
1/2 tsp. ground ginger
1/2 tsp. crushed red pepper
1/2 tsp. minced garlic

Combine ingredients in small saucepan and bring to boil over medium heat. Reduce heat to simmer and stir constantly for 1 to 2 minutes. Let cool.

Teriyaki Marinade:

8 tablespoons honey
4 tablespoons soy sauce
8 tablespoons ketchup
1 tsp. black pepper
1/2 tsp. ground ginger
1/2 tsp. minced garlic

Combine in bowl and blend well with wire whisk or fork. Cover cooked chicken wings with marinade and heat in 325 degree oven for 5 minutes.

Sweet and Sour Sauce:

1 tablespoon cornstarch
1 tablespoon cold water
1/4 cup sugar
1/4 cup soy sauce
2 tsp. vinegar
1 tsp. minced garlic
1/2 tsp. ground ginger
1/2 tsp. black pepper

In saucepan, whisk cornstarch and cold water until blended. Add remaining ingredients and cook stirring constantly over medium heat until mixture thickens and bubbles. Remove from heat and cool.

MICHAELS TURKEY BURGERS

We were amazed at how a teenager chose turkey burgers over beef burgers, but both are equally good in this recipe if the beef is an excellent, lean quality.

Have the kids choose and assemble various toppings and serve them at the table for everyone to sample. (Suggestions below)

Makes 4 Burgers
<u>Ingredients:</u>
1 lb. ground turkey
1/4 cup finely chopped scallions
2 tablespoons Worcestershire sauce
1 tsp. dried parsley
1 tsp. salt
1 tsp. black pepper
4 whole wheat or white rolls or buns

<u>KIDS:</u> Combine all ingredients, except rolls, in a bowl and mix with clean hands until well blended (** wash hands after handling meat). Shape 4 patties into thick burgers.

<u>ADULTS:</u> Place burgers on grill or fry pan and cook on medium low flame 6 to 8 minutes on each side or until no longer pink in center. Serve on rolls or buns.

SUGGESTED TOPPINGS:
Shredded or sliced American cheese
Sliced mozzarella or provolone
Lettuce
Sliced tomatoes
Pickles
Sliced red onions
Sliced mushrooms
Bacon bits

CONDIMENTS:
Ketchup
Mayonnaise
Honey Mustard
BBQ sauce
Russian or
Ranch dressing
Salsa
Guacamole

KATHERINES BOW-TIE PASTA WITH TOMATO SAUCE

The sauce can be made well in advance, tightly sealed and frozen until ready to use, or refrigerated for three days. Heat well before using.

Serves 4
Ingredients:
Tomato Sauce:
1/2 cup extra virgin olive oil
1/2 cup chopped onion
2 8 ounce cans tomato sauce
2 tablespoons tomato paste
1 cup water
1/2 tsp each basil and oregano
1 tsp. salt
1/2 tsp. black pepper

Adult Helpers: Heat oil in saucepan. Add onions and cook slowly, stirring often for 10-15 minutes on simmer.

KIDS: Stir remaining ingredients in a large bowl until well blended.

Adult Helpers: Add blended sauce to pan with cooked onion and stir well. Bring mixture to boil and simmer, covered, on low flame for approximately 30 minutes stirring occasionally.

To 5 quarts of boiling water in a large pot, add 1 lb. Bow-tie pasta and cook uncovered, stirring often, 8-10 minutes or until desired tenderness. Drain; serve immediately with sauce.

Tip: Serve with a healthy green salad and a basket of fresh assorted French or Italian breads, rolls and breadsticks.

ENJOY!!!

GREGORYS TURKEY SUBS

Kids have so much fun when assembling their own sandwiches and they have great ideas. You can use any deli meat and cheese for this sub sandwich. Greg chose turkey because it's his favorite.

Smart Boy!!!

INGREDIENTS:
Sliced turkey meat
Sliced Swiss cheese
Green leaf lettuce or spinach leaves, shredded
Sliced tomatoes
Sliced red onions (optional)
Sliced pickles
Mustard, mayo or use our vinaigrette (recipe follows)
Hoagie rolls or other sandwich rolls
Salt and pepper to taste

INGREDIENTS FOR SUB VINAIGRETTE:
1/2 cup extra virgin olive oil
1/4 cup red wine vinegar
1 tsp. dried parsley
1 tsp. dried oregano
Salt and pepper to taste

Mix all ingredients in a small bowl and whisk until well blended.
Store remaining vinaigrette in a covered container and refrigerate.
Assemble sandwich in layers and sprinkle with vinaigrette, if using.

LORINS MAC & CHEESE

Our Cuisine Alà Kids hostess has her own special recipe for this favorite kids dish. It's her topping that makes it so tasty.

Serves 4

INGREDIENTS:

1 lb. box elbow macaroni or small shells
2 cups shredded cheddar
1 stick unsalted butter
1/3 cup all purpose flour
2 1/2 cups whole milk or light cream
6 slices white or whole wheat bread, crumbled
4 tablespoons melted butter
5 quarts boiling water (salted optional)

Adult Helpers:

Add macaroni to boiling water and cook according to package directions or until tender. Drain in colander and return to pot. In a small saucepan melt unsalted butter and add flour whisking until blended. Cook and stir over low flame for 1 minute, then slowly add milk or cream and continue stirring until mixture thickens. Add shredded cheese and blend well. Pour sauce over macaroni in pot and stir well to mix.

Kids:

Butter a 2-quart baking dish. Combine pasta with cheese mixture in dish and mix well. Make topping. In separate bowl combine breadcrumbs with melted butter until breadcrumbs are coated. Sprinkle on top of macaroni until well covered.

Bake in 325-degree oven for approximately 20-25 minutes until golden brown.

KATIES SPAGHETTI AND MEATBALLS

Katie loves her mom's spaghetti and meatballs. Here is a recipe kids can really get into.

Serves 4-6
INGREDIENTS FOR ITALIAN MEATBALLS:
4 slices white bread, soaked in 1 cup water for 1 minute in a deep dish or bowl
2 eggs
1 lb. ground lean beef
1/2 cup grated Parmesan cheese
2 tablespoons fresh chopped parsley
2 tablespoons fresh chopped mint
1 tsp. salt
1 tsp. dried oregano
Dash pepper
Flour for coating

<u>KIDS:</u> With moist hands, mix all ingredients in large bowl and form mixture into approximately 24 small balls. Place flour on platter and roll meatballs until coated. Set aside.

<u>Adult helper:</u> Heat 1-inch vegetable oil in skillet until hot. Lower heat and brown meatballs, a few at a time. Drain on paper towels.

For our spaghetti sauce, we used our tomato sauce recipe (see pg. 14) or you may use your own favorite marinara sauce. Heat sauce in large pot and add meatballs. Simmer on low flame until meatballs are heated through.

Make 1 lb. spaghetti according to package directions, drain and serve with meatballs, sauce and grated or sliced parmesan cheese.

<u>Suggestion:</u> We love our garlic bread recipe with this menu.

MATTHEWS CHOCOLATE AND VANILLA PUDDING PARFAIT

Kids will love making this dessert. Adults should supervise with electric beaters and pudding directions.

Use store bought instant puddings and follow manufacturer's directions. Make 1 package vanilla pudding in one bowl, then 1 package chocolate pudding in another bowl.

Alternate layers in pretty dessert dishes.

This recipe can be made early in the day and refrigerated until serving time.

Garnish with chocolate or vanilla wafer (or both) & whipped topping.

VICTORIAS AND CATHERINES GREEK BUTTER COOKIES

The girls love to help their Yia-Yia (Greek for Grandmother) with these traditional and delicious butter cookies.

INGREDIENTS:

1 lb. butter (softened)
3 cups of sugar
9 eggs
1/4 cup warm milk
2 tsp of vanilla
8 tsp baking powder
10-12 cups flour
Sesame seeds (optional)

Makes approximately 4 Dozen

Adult helper: Combine butter and sugar in an electric mixer and mix for 3 minutes on medium speed. Add 8 of the eggs and vanilla. Beat until fluffy. Add baking powder and milk and beat well. Stop mixer. Sift flour and add 2 cups of the flour to the mixture. Continue to beat on low to medium speed. Continue to add flour until dough is not as sticky and becomes pliable. Stop mixer and use your hands if desired to mold into big ball.

Kids: Cut dough in half and roll each piece on a floured surface with a rolling pin or your hands. Make desired shapes with cookie cutters of your choice. Place cookies on ungreased baking sheets 1 inch apart. Beat remaining egg with a fork and brush each cookie lightly then sprinkle with sesame seeds, if using. Bake cookies in 350-degree oven for approximately 15 minutes or until golden brown.

ATHENAS MINI PIZZAS

Like all kids, all ages, Athena loves pizza. We thought our variation might be more fun. Check with family members for their favorite toppings and make individual pizzas for each one or use your imagination to create your own.

Kids: Use ready-made pizza dough from your local market. Shape pizza dough into 2-inch balls and place on large baking sheet. Flatten each ball with floured hand or rolling pin. Leave edges a little raised so center is deeper. Use our tomato sauce recipe (see pg. 14) or canned tomato sauce and spread one to two tablespoons on prepared dough. Add a variety of toppings to please everyone.

Adult helper: Bake pizzas in pre-heated 400-degree oven until crust is golden and toppings are done. Approximately 15 – 20 minutes.

Topping Ideas:

Shredded Mozzarella, white american or jack cheese
Sliced mushrooms
Diced onions, peppers, tomatoes
Pepperoni
Diced Proscuitto or cooked ham
Sliced olives.
Oregano, parsley
Salt and pepper to taste

CHAPTER 2
BREAKFAST AND DINNER

Weekend breakfast with the family:

FRESH FRUIT PLATTER
STUFFED FRENCH TOAST
HONEY MICROWAVE BACON
BLUEBERRY STREUSEL "MUFFUNS"
FUN FRUIT SHAKE

FRESH FRUIT PLATTER

You can choose any fruit for your fresh fruit platter as long as it's ripe and seasonal. We chose sliced watermelon, honeydew, pineapple, cantaloupe, green grapes, strawberries and blueberries.

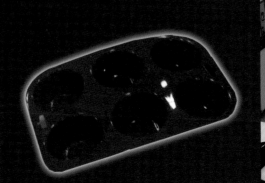

STUFFED FRENCH TOAST

Makes 8 triangles

INGREDIENTS:

1 8 ounce container whipped cream cheese
4 tablespoons raspberry jam (or jam of your choice)
8 slices white bread
2 eggs
1 cup of milk
1 tsp. vanilla extract

KIDS:

Spread cream cheese on 4 slices of bread and top with jam. Spread evenly. Place remaining 4 slices of bread on top of each of the first four to make four sandwiches.

Mix eggs, milk and vanilla extract in bowl and beat with wire whisk or fork, about 15-20 seconds.

Dip cream cheese and jam sandwiches, one a time, in egg mixture until coated on both sides. (Don't forget to wash your hands thoroughly after touching raw eggs.)

Adult helper:

Place prepared sandwiches on lightly greased griddle over medium high heat 2 minutes on each side or until golden brown. Remove from griddle when done and slice each sandwich diagonally in half. Place on platter and sprinkle with powdered sugar. Serve with maple or flavored syrup and butter if desired.

HONEY MICROWAVE BACON

A microwave bacon tray is a great investment. It makes cooking bacon easy and much safer than frying.

Place bacon strips on a microwave baking tray and drizzle with 1 tablespoon of honey. Cook bacon according to manufacturers directions.

BLUEBERRY STREUSEL "MUFFUNS"
Makes 12 Muffins

INGREDIENTS:
2 cups all purpose flour
2 tsp. baking powder
1/4 tsp. baking soda
1/4 tsp. salt
1/2 cup sugar
1 extra large egg, beaten
1cup whole milk
1/4 cup vegetable oil
1 1/2 cup fresh blueberries, rinsed and patted dry

STREUSEL TOPPING:
1 cup firmly packed brown sugar
1 cup all purpose flour
1/2 cup butter
2 tsp. cinnamon

Adult helper: For streusel, Combine all ingredients in food processor and set aside.

To make muffins:

Adult: Preheat oven to 350 degrees.
Kids: Grease a 12 cup muffin tin or use paper liners. Combine all ingredients except for blueberries in a medium bowl. Stir and blend well. Fold in fresh blueberries carefully. Spoon mixture into prepared muffin tin and sprinkle with streusel topping. Bake for 15-20 minutes or until golden.

Cool 10 minutes then remove from muffin tin carefully.

FUN FRUIT SHAKE

Makes 2 servings

INGREDIENTS:

1 cup fresh strawberries, washed, hulled and sliced
1 ripe banana, sliced
2 cups pineapple juice

In blender combine ingredients and puree until smooth. Pour in tall glasses and garnish with fruit of your choice.

One of the best things about family dinners is bringing everyone to the table. Togetherness and teamwork between parents and children creating fun and delicious meals can be memorable.

Our "kids speak out" team gave you plenty of delicious dinner ideas but we have a few more! We'd love you to try our fun and easy dinner menus, sure to please the whole family. Again, teamwork is the key! Everyone should have their (clean) hands in this one.

For dessert recipes on our dinner menus see chapter 4 – Yum-Yum desserts.

DINNER MENU #1:

Crunchy Oven Chicken

S'mashed potatoes

Candied Carrots

Fruit and Greens Salad

Rolls or Biscuits with butter

DESSERT:

Brownie Tarts with fresh berries with whipped cream

CRUNCHY MUNCHY OVEN CHICKEN CUTLETS

INGREDIENTS:

3 cups dry cornbread-stuffing mix
1/2-cup walnuts or almonds (optional)
1/2 cup of melted butter or margarine
1 tsp. garlic powder
1 tsp. salt
1/2 tsp. pepper
3 lbs. boneless chicken cutlets, washed and dried

ADULT HELPER:

In food processor, grind stuffing mix and walnuts or almonds, if using. Process until crumbs are fine. Set aside.

KIDS:

In a small bowl, combine next 4 ingredients. Dip chicken pieces one at a time, in butter mixture, then in stuffing mixture. Arrange chicken pieces on baking sheet and pour remaining butter mixture over chicken.

ADULT HELPER:

Bake at 350 degrees for 20-25 minutes or until done.

S'MASHED POTATOES

No peeling necessary! Kids will have fun doing the smashing! (And the eating)

INGREDIENTS:

1 lb medium or small red potatoes
1 cup of milk
1/2 stick of salted butter
Salt, pepper and fresh parsley to taste

KIDS:

Rinse red potatoes under cool water

ADULT HELPER:

Place potatoes in a large pot of boiling water and cook until fork tender. (About 20-30 minutes) Remove from pot and drain in colander. Place potatoes in a large bowl. Heat milk and butter until simmering. Set aside.

KIDS:

Take potato masher and smash the potatoes until just slightly lumpy.

ADULTS:

Add hot milk mixture and blend into potatoes. Add salt, pepper and parsley to taste.

CANDIED CARROTS:

Your local supermarket should carry peeled and cut carrot sticks or baby carrots.
(If not, peel 1 lb. fresh carrots and rinse well. Cut carrots in half diagonally and trim
ends or slice into 1 inch rounds.)

INGREDIENTS:

1 stick of unsalted butter
1/2 cup light brown sugar
1 tsp. ground cinnamon
1/2 tsp. ground cloves
1/4 cup maple syrup

KIDS:

Do the measuring and mix brown sugar, cinnamon and cloves in a bowl.

ADULTS:

Melt butter in a large skillet over low flame, then add brown sugar mixture and whisk
or blend well until smooth. Add maple syrup and stir. Place carrots in skillet and coat
well with mixture. Cook, covered on lowest flame for approximately 20 – 30 minutes or
until carrots are tender.

FRUIT AND GREENS SALAD:

INGREDIENTS:

1 head romaine lettuce
1 can approximately 11 ounces mandarin oranges
1 cup dried cranberries
1/2 cup of sunflower seeds

ADULTS:

Wash, dry and cut romaine lettuce into bite size pieces. Place in bowl. Drain mandarin oranges in colander and set aside.

Yogurt Dressing:

KIDS:

In a small bowl stir one 8-ounce container of plain yogurt with 2 tablespoons of honey and 1 teaspoon of ground cinnamon until well blended. Add drained mandarin oranges along with dried cranberries and sunflower seeds to romaine lettuce in bowl. Serve with dressing.

DINNER MENU # 2:

STUFF YOUR SOLE FACE

STUFFED FILET OF SOLE

GINGER RICE

GARLIC AND PARMESAN BREAD

BEANS AND VEGETABLE SALAD

DESSERT:

FUN-DO FONDUE

STUFFED FILET OF SOLE

Fish filets are generally boneless. Make sure the ones you buy have no small bones.

INGREDIENTS:

1/2 cup melted butter with two tablespoons lemon juice
4 sole filets (boneless)
salt and pepper to taste
1/4 cup chopped fresh dill
1/4 cup chopped fresh parsley
1/4 cup chopped chives or scallions
1 tomato, seeded and diced
1/4 cup shredded mozzarella
1/4 cup shredded provolone

KIDS:

With pastry brush, evenly coat each filet with melted butter and lemon juice. Salt and pepper to taste. Evenly spread chopped dill, parsley, chives or scallions and tomatoes on each filet. Top with shredded cheeses and roll or fold filet to close. Place filets on lightly sprayed or greased baking pan. Make fish faces.

ADULTS:

Bake filets at 350 degrees for approximately 15-20 minutes or until fish flakes easily. Garnish with lemon slices.

Fish Face suggestions:
Olives for eyes
Carrots for nose
Red pepper strips for mouth

WHITE RICE WITH FRESH GINGER

INGREDIENTS:

1 cup long grain white rice
2 1/4 cups water or chicken broth
2 tsp. butter
1/2 tsp. salt
2 tsp. peeled fresh ginger chopped fine or grated

ADULT:

Bring water or broth to boil. Add rice, butter, salt and fresh ginger. Reduce to simmer and cover pot. Cook until done, about 15-20 minutes.

HOMEMADE GARLIC PARMESAN BREAD

INGREDIENTS:

One whole Italian or French loaf
Four tablespoons melted butter
Two tablespoons garlic powder
One tablespoon grated parmesan cheese

ADULTS:

Slice whole loaf length wise in half.

KIDS:

Spread butter evenly on each side of both halves. Sprinkle garlic powder and parmesan evenly over butter. Close loaf and wrap bread in aluminum foil.

ADULTS:

Bake at 350 degrees for approximately 10-15 minutes

BEANS AND VEGETABLE SALAD

A different and healthy side dish for everyone.

INGREDIENTS:

1/2 cup each diced yellow and red pepper
1/2 cup grape tomatoes (halved)
1 can chickpeas, drained and rinsed
1 can red kidney beans, drained and rinsed
1/4 cup balsamic vinegar
1/8 cup of extra virgin olive oil
1/2 tsp. sugar
Salt and pepper to taste
Fresh chopped parsley to garnish

ADULT:

Prepare first 4 ingredients. Place in bowl.

KIDS:

Prepare dressing. In small bowl, combine vinegar, olive oil, sugar and salt and pepper to taste. Pour over bean mixture and garnish with fresh parsley.

DINNER MENU # *3*

IT'S "CHILI" OUT THERE

HOMEMADE CHILI
CORN BREAD MADELINES
NACHOS SUPREME

DESSERT:
BANANA SURPRISE

HOMEMADE CHILI

INGREDIENTS:

2 tablespoons vegetable oil
1/2 cup chopped onion
1 lb. lean ground beef or ground turkey
1 lb. can crushed or diced tomatoes with juice
1 15 ounce can red or pink beans drained
1/4 cup diced yellow, orange, red or green peppers
2 tsp. chili powder
1 package of shredded cheddar cheese

ADULTS:

In a skillet cook onions over medium heat in vegetable oil until soft, about 2-3 minutes. Add meat and brown, stirring often. Add tomatoes, beans, chopped peppers and chili powder and blend well. Reduce heat and simmer, covered, for about 25-30 minutes, stirring often. Top each serving with shredded cheese and serve with corn bread madelines and/or nachos supreme.

CORN BREAD MADELINES

A new shape for an old favorite. If you don't have a Madeline pan you can substitute a greased or paper lined muffin pan.

Makes 12 Madelines or 12 small muffins

INGREDIENTS:

1 1/2 cup all purpose flour, sifted
1/2-cup sugar
1/2 cup cornmeal
1 tsp. baking powder
1/2 tsp. salt
3/4 cup milk (whole preferred)
1 stick unsalted butter, melted in the microwave
2 eggs

KIDS:

Grease pans and set aside. With your adult helper, place dry ingredients in a bowl. Stir the flour, sugar, cornmeal, baking powder and salt until combined.

In another bowl, whisk the milk, melted butter and eggs.

With electric beater on low speed, pour the milk batter into the dry ingredients and mix just until blended.

Spoon batter into prepared pan and bake at 350 degrees until golden brown or until toothpick inserted comes out clean. Approximately 10-15 minutes.

Beverage Ideas for the Dinner Table

•Keep a pitcher of ice water on the table and add cut fresh lemons and/or limes.

•How about a pitcher of lemonade over-ice with fresh-cut strawberries (pass drinking straws for smaller children to avoid choking)

•Another idea is a pitcher of apple juice with cinnamon sticks

You could try a combination of your favorite dinnertime beverages and fun additions

CHAPTER 3
LUNCH & LUNCHBOX

Kids:

Whether you're eating lunch at the kitchen table or packing a lunchbox and thermos, you don't have to eat the same things day in and day out. Even the pickiest eaters have a wide range of choices. We've included some different lunch ideas with serving suggestions. Have fun changing them around or adding your own ideas.

*Recipes included

Menu 1:

*Peanut Butter & Jelly Cutouts (see Sandwich Cut-outs)
Banana
Chocolate chip cookies
Apple or Fruit juice

Menu 2:

*Chicken cutlet hero
(Place leftover crunchy oven chicken cutlets on hero bread with mayo, lettuce and sliced tomatoes or toppings of your choice.)
*Red Potato salad
Green Grapes
Milk

Menu 3:

* Homemade Chili (in thermos) with tortilla chips
Brownies
Lemonade or Limeade

Menu 4:

Portable Cheese Platter
(Place in plastic air-tight container or plastic seal-tight bags. A variety of sliced cheeses, pepperoni, salami, ham, crackers, and fresh fruit.)

Vanilla Yogurt
Bottled water or Fruit juice

Menu 5:

*Chicken & vegetable soup in thermos
Egg salad on whole wheat bread sandwich
*Oatmeal &golden raisin cookies
Milk or fruit juice

Menu 6:

*Tuna salad Wrap
Carrot sticks
Pudding snacks
Apple juice

Menu 7:

Ham & cheese on white or rye bread
*Corkscrew pasta salad
Apple or Orange
Milk or fruit juice

RED POTATO SALAD

Ingredients:

10 red potatoes
1/2 cup Buttermilk
1/3-cup mayonnaise
1 tablespoon white wine vinegar
Chopped fresh parsley (optional)

Adults:
Boil red potatoes until fork-tender. Drain potatoes in a colander and rinse with cold water. Set aside to cool.

Kids:
In a small bowl, whisk buttermilk, mayonnaise and vinegar until well blended. Set aside.

Adults:
When cooled, cut each potato in quarters and place in a medium bowl.

Kids:
Place dressing on potatoes and toss potatoes until well blended.

Can be served warm or cold.

TUNA SALAD WRAPS

Ingredients for Tuna Salad:

1 6-ounce can tuna, drained
2 tablespoons chopped celery
2 teaspoons chopped onion
1 teaspoon fresh lemon juice
2 tablespoons mayonnaise
Salt and pepper to taste
Flour Tortilla wraps

Kids:

Combine all ingredients and place about 2-3 tablespoons of tuna salad in center of tortilla wrap. Wrap both sides of tortilla towards the middle and tuck and secure each end.

Adults:

Slice wraps in half and wrap in plastic wrap to keep in place.

Repeat for more wraps.

CORKSCREW PASTA SALAD

Ingredients:

2 large tomatoes
10-ounce package of frozen baby peas
2-3 tablespoons of olive oil
salt and pepper to taste
1 lb of tri-color corkscrew pasta (or any tri-color pasta)
fresh chopped parsley

Adults:
Cut tomatoes in half and remove pulp. Dice tomatoes and set aside. Cook 1 lb of tri-color pasta in 5 qts. of boiling water until tender, stirring often. Drain pasta in colander & rinse with cold water.

Kids:
While still in colander, toss tomatoes, peas and olive oil into pasta and mix well.

Place prepared pasta in a pretty bowl or dish and sprinkle with chopped fresh parsley.

Serves 6-8

CHAPTER 4
YUM-YUM DESSERTS

DON'T DESERT DESSERT!!!

Kids (and adults) love dessert!!! Our junior chefs gave us their favorites. No counting calories on these yummy treats.

LORINS VANILLA EVERTHING SUNDAE

You've heard of chocolate lovers. Well our junior chef is a true vanilla lover. She even has her own sundae recipe and wants to share it with other vanilla fans.

INGREDIENTS:
A triple scoop of vanilla ice cream
White chocolate sauce (recipe follows)
Vanilla sprinkles
Vanilla whipped cream (see pg. 78)
Vanilla wafer or cookie
White chocolate, shavings to garnish
White chocolate cherry

Scoop ice cream into dessert dish or bowl, top with white chocolate sauce, add sprinkles, top with whipped cream and decorate with white chocolate shavings and cookie. ENJOY!!!

To make white chocolate cherry: Melt white chocolate in microwave safe bowl for 1 minute at half power and stir. Drain maraschino cherry on paper towel and pat dry. Dip the cherry into the chocolate and set on a piece of wax paper to harden.

INGREDIENTS FOR WHITE CHOCOLATE SAUCE:
1 cup of whipping cream (heavy cream)
8 1-ounce square white chocolate
2 tablespoons light corn syrup

Adult helpers: Cook whipping cream in a small heavy saucepan over low heat until heated, stirring often. Add white chocolate and corn syrup. Heat and stir until chocolate melts. Cool slightly.

NICOLES CHOCOLATE EVERYTHING SUNDAE

The ultimate chocolate sundae created by your ultimate chocolate lover.

INGREDIENTS:
A triple scoop of chocolate ice cream
Milk chocolate sauce (recipe follows)
Crumbled chocolate cookies
Chocolate whipped cream (see pg. 78)
Chocolate shavings
Chocolate covered strawberry

Scoop ice cream into a pretty dessert dish. Top with chocolate fudge sauce, crumbled cookies and chocolate whipped cream. Garnish with chocolate shavings and chocolate covered strawberry. AWESOME!!!

Make chocolate covered strawberry: Melt chocolate in a microwave safe bowl for 1 minute at half power. Stir well. Wash and dry strawberry. Dip in melted chocolate and set on wax paper until hardened.

INGREDIENTS FOR MILK CHOCOLATE SAUCE:
1 cup of heavy cream
2 tablespoons sugar
1 tablespoons unsalted butter
5 ounces milk chocolate finely chopped

Place chocolate in a medium bowl.

Adult helpers: In a small saucepan combine the cream, sugar and butter. Bring just to a boil over low-medium heat, stirring. Pour over the finely chopped milk chocolate in bowl and whisk gently until chocolate is melted and smooth and cool slightly.

FLAVORED WHIPPED CREAMS:

Vanilla whipped cream:

1 cup cold heavy cream
2 tablespoons confectioners' sugar
1 teaspoon vanilla extract
Place clean and dry mixing bowl and beaters in freezer for 10 minutes. Combine ingredients in the bowl and whip with beaters until stiff peaks form. Refrigerate after using.

Chocolate whipped cream:

1 cup cold heavy cream
3 tablespoons unsweetened cocoa
1/3 cup confectioners' sugar
1 tsp. vanilla extract
Pinch of salt

Combine ingredients in clean, dry bowl, chill in refrigerator at least 1 hour, or until very cold, then whip until stiff.

To make chocolate shavings lightly run a vegetable peeler across a block of chocolate at cool room temperature.

For wide chocolate curls slightly soften a block of chocolate then run a vegetable peeler along the slightly softened edge. You may have to experiment with the temperature of the chocolate to get it right.

BROWNIE TARTS WITH FRESH BERRIES:

Use your favorite brownie mix or recipe for this dessert.

Kids:
Make the batter according to manufacturer's directions. Place paper baking cups in a 12 cup muffin tin. Pour batter evenly into baking cups.

Adults:
Bake brownies according to manufacturer's directions. Remove tarts from oven and cool completely. When cooled, remove brownies from pan. Serve with an assortment of sliced berries in season and fresh whipped cream.

OATMEAL, CHOCOLATE CHIP & GOLDEN RAISIN COOKIES

INGREDIENTS:

1 cup butter, softened
1 1/4 cup brown sugar
1/2 cup sugar
2 eggs
2 tablespoons milk
2 teaspoons vanilla or chocolate extract
1 3/4 cups flour, sifted
1 tsp baking soda
2 1/4 cups dry oatmeal
1 12-ounce package milk chocolate chips
1 cup golden raisins

Adult:
Preheat oven to 350 degrees

Kids:
With an electric mixer (under adult supervision) or by hand, beat butter and both sugars until well blended and creamy. Add eggs, milk and either vanilla or chocolate extract and mix well. Add next five ingredients and blend well. On non-greased cookie sheet drop spoonfuls of dough, one at a time, about one inch apart.

Adults:
Bake in 350 degrees oven for about 10-15 minutes or until done.

BANANA SURPRISE

Kids:

In clear dessert dishes, alternate layers of prepared vanilla pudding, thawed whipped topping, sliced bananas and milk chocolate or white chocolate (or both) chips.

Top with whipped topping and chocolate chips.

FUN-DO FONDUE

1 store bought Pound Cake cut in cubes
   or
1 package of ladyfingers
   (or both)

An assortment of sliced fruit such as:
   Strawberries, Bananas, Peaches, Pineapple, Melons

1 package of large marshmallows

Place cakes, fruit and marshmallows on large platter. Place small bowls of dipping sauces in the middle and serve the forks. See photo on page 97.

SO MUCH FUN!!!!

APRICOT DIPPING SAUCE

1 12oz. jar of apricot preserves

1 Tablespoon of Apricot Nectar or Apple Juice

<u>Kids:</u>
Mix ingredients in a microwave-safe bowl. Cover with plastic wrap.

<u>Adults:</u>
Heat mixture in microwave for 30-45 seconds. Stir, let cool, serve.

RASPBERRY DIPPING SAUCE

1 10 oz. package of frozen raspberries
2 Tablespoons of sugar or sugar to taste
1 Tablespoon of Apple Juice

<u>Kids:</u>
Place ingredients in jar of blender.

<u>Adults:</u>
Puree mixture until smooth for about 10 seconds. Pour into Microwave-safe bowl and heat in microwave for 30 – 45 seconds. Stir, let cool and serve.

CHOCOLATE SAUCE

1 12 oz. package of milk chips
1/4 cup of milk

Place chips in microwave-safe bowl and heat in microwave at 50% power for 1 minute or until soft. Add 1/4 cup of milk and whisk until smooth. Add milk as needed for dipping consistency.

(Caution: mixture will be hot) Serve while warm.

CHAPTER 5
A BIRTHDAY PARTY

PARENTS & ADULT HELPERS:

Planning the "perfect" birthday party for your child is challenging at best. A lot of parents choose to have these parties in places other than the home and that is fine. But whether you decide to have it at home or out, the treats you serve are always an issue, especially to the children. While pizza, hot dogs and burgers are proverbial favorites, there is a fun alternative. We would like to share our version of the "perfect" birthday menu, Cuisine Alà Kids style!

SIMPLE & FUN!!!!!

BIRTHDAY MENU:

Sandwich Cut-outs

Veggie Chips & Pretzels

DYO Cupcakes

Chocolate Lollipop Favors

Party Punch

SANDWICH CUTOUTS

These can be made early on the day of the party. They are lots of fun to make so have the birthday child help.

<u>You'll need:</u>

A variety of cookie cutters (different sizes and shapes)

Cold Cuts such as ham, turkey, American and/or Swiss cheese

Tuna Salad
Egg Salad

Peanut butter & Jellies

Assorted sliced breads such as white, rye or whole wheat

Mayonnaise and mustard (optional)

Assemble a variety of sandwiches. Using cookie cutters, make different shapes from each sandwich. Spell the birthday childs name with alphabet cutters. They'll love it!

Place sandwich cutouts on platters, cover tightly with plastic wrap and refrigerate until party. Serve with small bowl of veggie chips and pretzels on side.

*DYO CUPCAKES:

*(Decorate your own)

   Your little party guests will love this idea. It creates a lot of fun and choices. The cupcakes can be made the day before the party and the toppings assembled the morning of the party. Serve a variety of flavors and watch the fun begin. It's amazing how creative kids can be, especially when they get to eat their works of art!

Photo of Kiki's Birthday Party

BIRTHDAY CUPCAKES:

Your local supermarket offers a variety of delicious and easy to make cake mixes and ready-made frostings to choose from. Or you can use our fabulous homemade cupcake recipes, which follow.

Have the birthday child do the measuring and mixing and adult helpers can do the baking.

Choose an assortment of cupcakes and toppings to please each little guest.

Always supervise and use caution with smaller children at the party.

VANILLA SUGAR-COOKIE CUPCAKES:

We call them this because these cupcakes form a sugary top similar to a cookie.
DEEEELICIOUS!!!!

Ingredients:

1/2-cup butter, softened
1 3/4 cups sugar
4 egg whites
2 1/2 teaspoons vanilla
2 1/4 cups flour, sifted
1-tablespoon baking powder
1/4-teaspoon salt
1-cup milk

Sugar for sprinkling

Adults: Preheat oven to 350 degrees

Kids: Line a 12 cup muffin tin with paper baking cups.

Adults: With an electric mixer at medium speed, cream butter and sugar until light. Add egg whites and vanilla; blend well. Add flour, baking powder, salt and milk, beating and blending well.

Kids: Pour batter into prepared pan, filling each tin halfway. Sprinkle added sugar on tops.

Adults: Bake in pre-heated 350 degrees oven for 20-25 minutes or until tops spring back. Let cool completely before serving.

Batter makes 20 medium size cupcakes.

HOT CHOCOLATE CUPCAKES

Our kid testers named these after their favorite hot winter drink. If you like, you can serve these with one of our homemade whipped creams

SUPER GOOD!!!!

Ingredients:
1/2-cup butter, softened
1 and 3/4 cup sugar
4 egg whites
2 teaspoons vanilla
2 cups flour, sifted
1/4 cup cocoa powder
1 tablespoon baking powder
1/4-teaspoon salt
1-cup milk

Adults: Preheat oven to 350 degrees

Kids: Line a 12 cup muffin tin with paper baking cups. Set aside.

Adults: With an electric mixer at medium speed, cream butter and sugar until light. Add egg whites and vanilla; blend well. Add flour, cocoa, baking powder, salt and milk beating and blending well.

Kids: Pour batter into prepared pan, filling each tin half to three quarters full.

Adults: Bake in preheated 350 degrees oven for 20-25 minutes or until tops spring back when pressed. Let cool completely before serving.

Makes approximately 18-20 medium size cupcakes

STRAWBERRY MILK CUPCAKES

Tastes like real strawberry milk. Kids love them!

<u>Ingredients</u>:

1/2-cup butter, softened
1 and 1/2 cup sugar
4 egg whites
2 1/2 teaspoons vanilla
2 cups flour
1/4 cup strawberry milk powder
1/4-teaspoon salt
1 tablespoon baking powder
1-cup milk

<u>Adults</u>: Preheat oven to 350 degrees

<u>Kids</u>: Line a 12 cup muffin tin with paper baking cups.

<u>Adults</u>: With an electric mixer at medium speed, cream butter and sugar until light. Add egg whites and vanilla; blend well. Add flour, strawberry powder, baking powder, salt and milk, beating and blending well.

<u>Kids</u>: Pour batter into prepared pan, filling each tin halfway.

<u>Adults</u>: Bake in preheated 350 degree oven for 20-25 minutes or until done. Let cool completely before serving.

Makes approximately 20 medium size cupcakes.

BANANA SHAKE CUPCAKES:

You'll go bananas over these.

Ingredients:

1/2 cup butter
1 3/4 cups sugar
2 large ripe bananas
4 egg whites
2 1/2 teaspoon vanilla
2 1/4 cups flour, sifted
1 tablespoon baking powder
1/4 teaspoon salt
1 cup milk

KIDS:
Cream butter and sugar until light and creamy. (If using an electric mixer make sure an adult supervises. Mash bananas and add to sugar and butter mixture, blending well.

Add remaining ingredients, beating well. Line 12 muffin tin cups with paper baking cups. Pour batter into prepared muffin pan, filling tins half to three quarters full.

ADULTS:
Bake cupcakes in pre-heated 350 degrees oven for 20-25 minutes or until top springs back when touched. Remove from oven and cool completely.

Place small bowls of assorted ready-made frostings and toppings on party table with plastic utensils and watch the fun. This is a party game in itself.

CUPCAKES:
Chocolate
Vanilla
Strawberry
Banana

TOPPINGS:
Chocolate sprinkles
Rainbow sprinkles
Tiny cake candies
Mini-marshmallows
M&M's

STORE BOUGHT FROSTINGS:
White
Chocolate
Lemon
Strawberry
Confetti

CHOCOLATE LOLLIPOP FAVORS:

These fun treats can be made one week before the party. Store wrapped lollipops in a dry cool area or refrigerate until party.

You will need:

14 ounces of milk chocolate
(Can use any color chocolate)
A lollipop plastic mold
Lollipop sticks
Plastic wrap
Ribbon

Adult Helper:

Melt chocolate in a microwave safe bowl at medium power for one minute. Stir. Melt again at medium power for 30 seconds. Check consistency of chocolate. If still hard, microwave in 10 second intervals.

Kid chefs:

With a spoon, pour melted milk chocolate in plastic molds filling them 3/4 full. Place lollipop sticks in tray, make sure to cover the tip of the stick with chocolate. Tap tray on counter once to loosen any air bubbles. Place tray in freezer for 10-15 minutes or until hard. Carefully remove lollipops and set aside. Repeat until you have enough favors.

Wrap each lollipop with plastic wrap and tie with party ribbons of your choice.

PARTY PUNCH:

In a punch bowl, mix equal parts cold cranberry juice and ginger ale. Add scoops of rainbow sherbet.

Serve in paper cups.

SPECIAL DEDICATIONS:

To my Katina, Lorin & Nicole - Thanks for all your hard work and for all the fun we had. I love you all.

Athena, Zena, & Kiki – Yia-Yia Loves You.

ABOUT THE AUTHOR

Janet Christon is the owner and chef of Zenovia Catering. For more than ten years, she has specialized in production, film, cable television catering as well as private catering and children's parties. As a mother of four and a grandmother of three, her favorite job is feeding her family and teaching them the art of cooking and baking.